CALIFORNIA

CALIFORNIA

CONTENTS

1713—1784

"No service is too great,
no service is too small
for the love of God
and man."

To the memory of Padre
Junipero Serra, whose
sandaled footprints in
California's dust are its
most enduring monuments,
this volume is respectfully
dedicated.

Library of Congress Catalog Card Number 72-122036

Copyright® 1970 by

Publisher • Charles H. Belding

Designer • Robert Reynolds

Text • David W. Toll

Printer • Graphic Arts Center

Bindery • Lincoln and Allen

Printed in the United States of America

Right: Statue of Padre Serra
surrounded by brilliant red
Bougainvillea in the garden of
Mission San Juan Capistrano.

Below: Moon climbs in the evening sky over downtown San Diego, viewed from the shores of Coronado.

Right: California State Building housing various museums in Balboa Park, San Diego, California. This graceful structure is considered to be the finest example of Spanish architecture in the United States.

Below: Panorama of San Diego Bay yacht harbor and downtown as seen from Point Lomas residential area.

Right: Colorful spinnakers create a spectacular picture as ocean class sailboats race before a good breeze. Air view over Pacific Ocean near Long Beach.

Below: Hundreds of colorful lights illuminate a major petroleum refinery near California oil field.

Right: Silent sentinel perched aside campanile of Mission San Gabriel, Alta California, the fourth mission founded by Padre Serra, September 8, 1771.

Below: Orange grove near Redlands. In the distance, winter snows on lofty San Bernardino Mountain. Brightly illuminated fountains decorate El Paseo Mall, Los Angeles Civic Center. In background, county Water and Power building always lighted at night. Ribbons of traffic weave together with the joining of San Bernardino and Long Beach freeways. In the distance, snowcapped ridges of 10,064 ft. Mt. Baldy.

Right: Santa Monica and Harbor freeways interchange bordering downtown Los Angeles skyline. New convention center under construction (left center) on 16.5 acre site. The main exhibit hall will seat 15,000 people for meetings, up to 8,000 for dinner.

Right: Laguna Beach, popular resort community midway between Los Angeles and San Diego on State Hwy. 1. In foreground, brilliant blooms of red aloe.

12   Ice plant blooms give appearance of mosaic carpet.

CALIFORNIA

July, 1769. His face is gray with pain and exhaustion, and sweat has eroded muddy streaks in the dust powdering his cheeks. His dry lips move ceaselessly in silent prayer as he stumbles and slides down the steep rocky side of the deep ravine. He alternately pulls his mule after him and hangs on to the halter rope for dear life as his feet dislodge small avalanches of loose stones and slip out from under him. At the shadowed bottom of the ravine he rests, wipes his forehead with the dingy cuff of his robe, and waits as his companions follow after him, slipping and cursing, sweating and red-faced, yanking their reluctant animals along. He is a small man, only a few inches more than five feet in height, and fifty-six years old. A leg infection troubles him constantly, yet his eyes are curiously serene as he watches their difficult downhill progress.

At length the small group of leather-jacketed soldiers and Christian neophytes from Loreto labors to the bottom of the ravine and stops in the shade to blow and rest. Outdistanced by the main body of men, they had set out six weeks earlier, traveling north through unexplored wilderness, and they are near exhaustion.

"But what does that matter now?" the small priest had written in his diary the night before. "We no longer feel the hardships of our journey; our hearts are filled with joy as we think of all the dear friends we shall clasp in our arms tomorrow."

They scramble up out of the ravine and stand for a moment on its lip, looking in vain out over the plain toward the sea for a glimpse of the main party. The Bay of San Diego lies within the embrace of a sandy arm extending up its seaward side from the south, and the brushy plain is striped with ravines through which the rains of winter flow down from the upper slopes. A few small hills poke up, but there are few trees except along the streambeds and on the higher elevations. Grapevines grow wild and the Rose of Castile is abundant. Rosemary and sage are commonplace in the sandy gray-brown soil. The Spaniards resume their progress toward the sea and rabbits skitter away at their approach. Antelope herds melt out of sight over the rolling hills.

The men make their way diagonally across the plain to reach shore near the mouth of the bay, and in four hours they are in sight of two ships lying at anchor there. In five they are standing on the sandy shore. Gulls, white against the brilliant blue of the sky, wheel and veer in dimwitted excitement and greet the tired men with shrill, reedy shrieks. A launch bobs toward shore from one of the ships, and the oarsmen direct them northward three miles. The men hurry on, a fluid body, each man alternately hurrying and slowing, like leaves blown along with the wind.

Despite his excitement and exultation, the lame priest is the last to reach the rough camp at the top of the knoll. His fellow missionaries run down the slope to embrace him, all but one who remains behind to complete the lean-to of branches and brush which will serve as a church. "It was a great day of rejoicing and merriment for all," the priest writes in his journal that evening, "because although each one in his respective journey had undergone the same hardships, their meeting through their mutual alleviation from hardship now became the material for mutual accounts of their experiences. And although this sort of consolation appears to be the solace of the miserable, for us it was the source of happiness.

"Thus was our arrival in health and happiness and contentment at the famous and highly desirable

> Port of San Diego
> -Praise Be To God-"

For Fray Junipero Serra, accustomed to seeing in everything the benign hand of God, the occasion may indeed have been wholly joyful. But for the other members of the Holy Expedition the small camp was overhung with dread and the odor of death.

For several years the energetic and ambitious Galvez had pressed for Spanish occupation of the little-known territory north of Baja California. It was territory long claimed for the Spanish crown, but there were other projects in New Spain, a territory extending from Chile to southern Arizona, of more pressing urgency and of better potential for financial return. But now the Russians had established trading posts and otter hunting colonies in the Aleutians, and Galvez used their presence to persuade Carlos III that Spanish claims to Alta California were in jeopardy. Accordingly, an expedition was formed to protect Spanish sovereignty by establishing an outpost at the harbor of Monterey, described more than 150 years earlier by Vizcaino as the best on the Pacific coast. A second settlement was to be established at San Diego. Missionaries were to convert and civilize the native population, and the military was to fortify the country against intrusion and protect the missionaries. Three ships departed the Mexican coast independently, each heavily laden with supplies: the *San Carlos,* the *San Antonio* and the *San Jose.* Two overland contingents traveled separately from Baja California. All elements of the expedition were to come together at San Diego.

The *San Antonio* was the first ship into harbor, but two of the crew had died at sea of scurvy and half of the remaining twenty-six were so badly afflicted they could not leave their hammocks. Eight more died at San Diego. The *San Antonio* had been riding uneasily at anchor for nearly three weeks when the *San Carlos* made port after 110 days at sea. Her crew was so scurvy-ridden that the few sailors still on their feet hadn't the strength to lower the sails or launch a boat. By the time Serra limped so eagerly into camp, only two of the sailors from the *San Carlos* were still alive. The *San Jose* was lost at sea with all hands. Three soldiers had died on the march, and numbers of the Indian neophytes had deserted. Already, with the toehold of empire only tenuously established at San Diego, almost 150 men are dead and many of the survivors are miserable with illness and injury.

The Indians in the vicinity, perhaps thirty-five or forty families, are fascinated with the Spaniards, especially with their clothing. Despite generous offers by the priests, who are anxious to attract the heathen to them, the Indians will not touch the Spaniards' food, probably because of the pitiful condition of so many members of the expedition. Soon enough the Spaniards are trading their extra clothing for the food the Indians can provide.

They can offer fish, game and wild plants and roots, but not the maize, squash or beans grown by the tribes along the Colorado far to the east, since those crops cannot survive the long dry summers without irrigation, and irrigation is unknown.

Portola, Governor of Baja California and comandante of the expedition, orders the San Antonio to return to Mexico for supplies, making up a crew of the surviving seamen and a few able-bodied soldiers. The ship sails July 9, and arrives in San Blas three weeks later with nine more dead. Five days after the San Antonio weighs anchor, Portola departs with more than sixty men to establish a base at Monterey. Serra and two other priests remain behind to tend the thirty-five invalids with the help of a few servants and muleteers and a guard of eight soldiers. On July 16 he erects a large white cross on the hilltop three miles from the harbor where the San Carlos is creaking dolefully at anchor, and sings mass in the brush shelter beneath it. Thus the first mission is established in California.

Portola's expedition plods slowly northward along the coast. He rides at the head of the column, and behind him trail a troop of soldiers, a work-gang of Indians with shovels and axes to clear the trail, four trains of twenty-five mules each, carrying provisions for six months, each with drovers and a guard of soldiers, and then the rearguard troop under the command of Captain Rivera, bringing with them the spare horses and mules. The column moved slowly, sometimes only a few hours a day because of the difficulty of the terrain and the uncertainty of finding water and feed for the animals in the arid land. They press north, rest, press on again over the green-seamed brown hills, always in sight of the foam-edged opal of the sea.

They encounter many Indians; short, brown-skinned people whose villages of hemispherical reed huts are concentrated along the coast and in the river valleys between the mountains and the sea. They welcome the Spaniards, feast and celebrate them, until the Spaniards grow sick of the taste of fish.

There are about 150,000 Indians in California, perhaps a third of them in the narrow coastal strip the Spaniards propose to occupy. So easy is it for these people to provide for themselves in this country that they require and have developed little of the formal social organization that has re-sulted in complex and interdependent Indian societies elsewhere in North America.

They need nothing from their neighbors except, occasionally, some richer land. For this they will fight, and for revenge against violence and the acts of witchcraft in which they profoundly believe, but their warfare seldom amounts to more than sudden ambushes and brief skirmishes in which the tools of the hunt and of the household are turned briefly to homicide. Only the Mojaves, the agriculturalists along the lower reaches of the Colorado, make tools—clubs —to be used exclusively as weapons.

The social isolation of Indian populations from one another is reflected in the diversity of their languages. Seven basic language stocks are represented in California, and these had been broken into twenty linguistic groups which had been splintered in turn into more than 130 local dialects. As a result, the language of one village is not likely to be understood even in the next, and without a common language and a tradition of co-operation, the Indians are ill-equipped to resist the Spanish intrusion in any concerted way even if they could grasp the implications of the Spanish advance. They dress themselves in bird-feather cloaks at the sight of the travelers, and offer gifts of food and entertainment.

Portola follows the scalloped coast to the barrier imposed by the Santa Lucia Mountains, crosses them under the deep-green canopy of oaks spread across their golden flanks, and drops back down to the sea at Monterey by following the Salinas River. But the great open crescent cannot be reconciled with Vizcaino's glowing description of a perfect natural harbor, and they continue north. After three and a half months of travel their way is blocked by an immense inlet, a vast landlocked harbor. At its mouth they see the Farralones and realize they have come too far. Disgusted, they turn back, and reach San Diego at the end of January, slaughtering their mules for food in the final stages of the march. Many of the soldiers are ill, and everyone has suffered from diarrhea. Portola must be carried on a litter. But no lives are lost.

The men left behind at San Diego have not fared so well. Eighteen more men are dead of scurvy, and one had been killed by Indians. And the San Antonio has not returned with supplies. Portola orders forty men to return overland to Baja California for cattle and supplies—and to relieve himself of the burden of feeding them from the dwindling stores. He determines to wait three weeks for the San Antonio, and to return to Mexico if she does not appear in that time. Serra objects. If the soldiers cannot secure the country for the king, he can still secure its people for God. If Portola goes, he will stay aboard the San Carlos to perform his holy mission. And on the afternoon of the last day of waiting the sails of a packet ship are sighted far out at sea. Four days later the San Antonio makes port with a cargo of provisions.

On April 16 the San Antonio puts to sea

again, bound this time for Monterey. Portola sets out again by land, this time taking only a small contingent of the strongest of his soldiers, and twenty-six men stay behind at San Diego: two priests, nine soldiers and fifteen Indians. On May 31 the land and sea elements of the expedition are reunited at Monterey where they are met by the local Indians who bring fresh-killed deer and antelope from the hills. Grasslands verge on the sandy shore where whales are sometimes washed ashore, and near the mouth of the Carmel River the reeds grow as high as a man on horseback. Seals caper beyond the surf.

On June 3 Serra and Portola dedicate the settlement site to the Faith and to the king with an accompaniment of bells, musket vollies and a salute of cannon from the *San Antonio*. They build three small buildings and on July 9, a few days more than a year after their arrival in Alta California, the men bound for Mexico, Portola among them, depart in the *San Antonio*.

Spanish California is established in the wilderness: two tiny hamlets 450 miles apart, entirely dependent for survival on sea-borne supplies from Mexico and the good will of the Indians. Galvez, in his official report, does not emphasize the difficulties. "God is with us," he writes, "and . . . it is He who has brought our undertaking to a successful issue."

March, 1806. The ship *Juno,* a month out of Sitka, creeps through the wisps of fog at the entrance to San Francisco Bay and slides with the surging tide in a slow turn to starboard.

"What ship are you?" The hail bounces across the gently slopping swells from a small fortification on the shore.

"The ship *Juno*, Russian, from Sitka!"

There is a moment's silence. "Come about! Drop anchor here near the fortress and send a boat ashore!"

In reponse the Russian sailors begin hauling clumsily at the sail. Their efforts are so slow that when the ship at last loses way, and the anchor is cast into the sea, the ship lies beyond the range of the Spanish cannon. The *Juno's* longboat is lowered over the side, and fifteen or twenty Spanish horsemen gallop furiously to the shore, capes streaming out behind them, and wheel their horses to a dramatic halt at the water's edge. They wait in a nervously shifting cluster as the Russian sailors haul at their oars to bring the boat gliding across the slate-gray surface of the bay. A priest on muleback comes bumping down to join the horsemen at a spleen-bursting trot, his sandaled heels thumping against the mule's ribs with each step.

Lt. Davidov and Dr. Langsdorff clamber out of the boat and walk toward the dismounting horsemen as the boatmen and the crew of the *Juno,* gathered at the rail, watch expectantly. A young Spaniard, wearing a red serape and intricately stitched boots, makes a slight, formal bow and introduces himself in Spanish. Langsdorff replies in Russian. The Spaniard smiles

apologetically, makes an elaborate shrug and shakes his head. Langsdorff repeats himself in French. It is not understood. German is no better, nor English, nor Portuguese. At last Langsdorff addresses the priest in Latin, and the priest replies. The conversation proceeds: Dr. Langsdorff to Fray Jose Uria in Latin, and Fr. Uria in Spanish to Don Luis Arguello, First Lieutenant of the Royal Presidio of San Francisco and the son of its temporarily absent comandante.

The *Juno,* Langsdorff explains carefully, is commanded by Lt. Khvostov of the Imperial Russian Navy, and carries the Czar's Plenipotentiary, Nicholas Rezanov, who has only recently returned from a mission of state to Japan and has been visiting the Russian settlements in Alaska. The ship was bound for Monterey where he had planned a formal visit, when bad weather had caused some damage to the *Juno* and had reduced their provisions to the danger point. They had put into San Francisco to make the necessary repairs and, hopefully, to reprovision the vessel. Langsdorff waits impassively as his explanation is relayed to the young commander. Arguello asks why there is but one small ship instead of the two larger ones they had been led to expect, and Langsdorff concocts an answer that satisfies him. Except for the fact of Rezanov's presence aboard the *Juno,* every word of Langsdorff's is a lie.

Arguello scarcely hesitates. He invites Rezanov ashore. Davidov and Langsdorff climb back into the boat and return to the *Juno,* and several of the Spaniards leap back up on their horses and race back to the Presidio. When Rezanov, resplendent in his green court uniform, steps lightly ashore, these men have returned with extra horses.

Formal greetings are exchanged and Rezanov mounts one of the horses, Langsdorff and Davidov climbing up on others. In the center of the group of Spaniards, the Russians are convoyed to the walled cluster of low buildings that is the Royal Presidio of San Francisco.

It is a most unmilitary place, this Presidio. For one thing there are only forty soldiers, and they are scattered between the presidio itself, the mission an hour's ride away to the southwest, the battery under the red cliffs at the harbor entrance, and another battery farther south down the coast. For another thing, it is scrupulously clean. The adobe walls, seven feet thick and fifteen feet high are whitewashed to a blinding whiteness, and the severely plain architecture of the single-story buildings inside the enclosure is embellished almost romantically by the clambering growth of Rose of Castile. The dirt floor of the courtyard has been carefully swept. And for a third, the women seem quite gentle and well-bred, a decided contrast to their counterparts in most military camps.

The Russians are ushered into the Arguello family quarters, a small warren of rooms, bare-walled and dirt floored, with a few Indian-made reed mats and rough-hewn pieces of furniture to relieve the monastic simplicity. And yet the almost primitive quality of the living arrangements is contradicted when the guests are served a welcoming breakfast on the most elaborately worked silver they had seen outside the Imperial Court at St. Petersburg.

Rezanov has not seen St. Petersburg for a long time. And though he is careful not to show it, the hearty meal provided by the Spaniards fills his belly for the first time in many months. For in fact there is barely any food aboard the *Juno,* which had been purchased with cargo and crew from her Yankee captain, and Rezanov's visit to San Francisco is a desperate, last-ditch gamble to save the starving Alaskan colonies.

At the hunting settlements they have left behind are only the skeletal remains of a once-vigorous Russian-American Company. The settlers are dying of malnutrition and exposure in ill-thatched, unheated huts. There are more sick than well, and the settlements had been scoured of the strongest men to crew the *Juno.* Several of them had died in the journey south. Without supplies, the colonies are doomed, and Rezanov has come, despite the well-known Spanish interdiction on foreign trade, to save them with supplies from California. He sailed on February 25. Four weeks later, after an unsuccessful attempt to enter the mouth of the Columbia, the *Juno* passed Cape Mendocino abeam to port. The dense pine forests of the northwest coast gave way to soft-shouldered sea cliffs, an empty and inhospitable shoreline despite the furry cover of fresh grass on the hills, and the Russians commented gloomily among themselves that there was no hint of smoke anywhere to indicate the presence of man.

In spite of their forebodings, their welcome by the Spaniards is genuinely warm and gracious, and the Russians are captivated by the easy generosity of these people. Still, Rezanov does not neglect to make a careful study of the harbor and land defenses. If the Spaniards refuse to trade willingly, it may be necessary to take what is needed by force.

A few miles to the southwest of the presidio is the Mission, and the path between them crosses open sand hills capable of supporting only low shrubs, birds, and a few rabbits. There are some 1,200 Indian neophytes quartered in eight large barracks-like buildings behind the main compound. Three or four soldiers are assigned to protect the three padres. The unmarried women and girls live in an enclosed compound which the priests lock at night and spend their days weaving woolen blankets for use by the neophyte population. The men tend the vegetable gardens and the grain fields, and gather in the forty to fifty cattle required each week for the stew which is the staple diet provided by the missionaries.

There are nineteen such missions in California, and four presidios with which to protect them. Serra is long dead, and his pupil and successor, Lasuen. The present Padre-Presidente of the missions, Fr. Estevan Tapis, has moved his headquarters from the Mission San Carlos Borromeo on the Carmel

River for the balmier climate of Santa Barbara. Communication between the Spanish establishments is by horseback and the monthly coastal packet bringing mail and supplies from Mexico. News from the capital at Mexico City is two months old by the time it reaches the California settlements, and news from Europe is six months out of date. The missions have a few solid-wheeled *carretas* that squeal along behind paired oxen for hauling grain and supplies. No one ventures far from the settlements by foot; the half-wild bulls of the mission herds will chase a man down and kill him. So numerous are these animals that only a few weeks before Rezanov's arrival 20,000 of them have been rounded up and slaughtered to prevent overgrazing.

The Indians between San Diego and San Francisco are pacified. The few who still live in their ancestral villages, old people for the most part, are docile and content to be left in peace in the wreckage of their old ways. The neophyte population numbers about 20,000. They and the villagers alike are stricken with periodic epidemics. Measles, syphilis and the common cold have already killed tens of thousands, and the onset of sickness produces such dispirit among them that they seem to die as much from the suggestion of sickness as from the sickness itself.

The Spaniards venture only occasionally into the interior, where large numbers of hostile Indians control the broad valley and marshlands and the foothills of the Sierra Nevada. One such expedition, composed of a sergeant, a corporal and thirteen men, return from scouting the region while Rezanov is in San Francisco. They report finding a fertile country, heavily populated, thickly forested and well watered by rivers and streams, but nothing which offers any urgent reason for colonization: no sophisticated indigenous civilization, no industry, no easy route to Santa Fe, no gold. Their report is filed as a matter of interest only.

Far to the south, at the Mission San Gabriel, the priests have managed to coax a few grapevines into production and are experimenting with orange trees. The nearby pueblo of Los Angeles, founded twenty-five years earlier by forty-six settlers of mixed background, has suffered from lack of water, unsophisticated agricultural techniques and the general prohibition against trade. At San Diego, despite the government ban, an occasional Boston trader makes port and attempts a clandestine trade in hides and tallow. At the pueblo of San Jose, however, the population has grown from one hundred settlers twenty years previously, to about seven hundred. Fruit trees are bearing abundantly, vineyards deliver up grapes like those at Malaga, and grain bursts up out of the rich soil without requiring much care. The only disadvantage is the lack of timber, but nearby chalk hills and natural clay deposits provide the materials for adobe brick of good quality.

Monterey, still the capital, is an undistinguished collection of cramped buildings, although California's only physician is headquartered there. The mission has long been removed from the vicinity of the presidio to reduce the friction between the priests and the military and civil authorities, and to diminish the pernicious influence of the soldiers on the manners and morals of the neophytes. In all of California there are still fewer than two thousand non-Indians.

With trade forbidden, these people rely upon the produce of the missions and pueblos for their principal wants, and upon the packet ships from Mexico for what they cannot grow or make for themselves. Yet in spite of the limitations, the missions already produce more than is needed to sustain the population, and there is no outlet for this surplus. Moreover, the supplies furnished from Mexico are often meagre and ill-chosen, and the missionaries at San Francisco are fascinated with the gifts of cloth-of-gold and linen with which Rezanov presents them. He has seen their full granaries, and he sees their quickened interest in the *Juno's* cargo of manufactured goods.

Governor Arrillaga rides overland from Monterey with Don Luis Arguello, comandante of the San Francisco presidio, and Don Jose De la Guerra, comandante of the Monterey presidio. Despite age and illness he prefers to make the difficult journey himself rather than allow Rezanov to see the inadequate defenses of the capital. He also sends a detachment of soldiers to the mission at Santa Clara, where they will be more readily available in case of emergency.

There is no emergency except that aboard the *Juno*, where the sailors make inevitable comparisons between the provisions furnished by the Spaniards and those available back at Sitka. Three Boston sailors and a Prussian ask Rezanov for permission to leave the crew, and he has them taken under guard in a skiff to Alcatraz where they remain in isolation for the duration of the *Juno's* visit. The remainder of the crew is kept aboard under heavy guard, but despite every precaution, seamen Kalianin and Polkanov manage to escape from a laundry detail and desert.

Rezanov assures Governor Arrillaga that the Czar has no territorial ambitions in Spanish California and that, indeed, such a plan would be impractical since it would require heavy cost to fortify and defend a colony, more cost than the benefit could be expected to repay. What he wants, *all* he wants, he insists, is an opportunity to establish a mutually beneficial trade. Arrillaga agrees that trade would be productive for California, but insists that it is impossible in the face of the government ban. Rezanov desists.

Soon enough, however, he announces his betrothal to Senorita Maria de la Concepcion Arguello, and Arrillaga can refuse him no longer. Under a complex system of payment which avoids the appearance of a direct trade, Arrillaga authorizes the padres at San Francisco and San Jose to bring the provisions Rezanov needs.

His marriage to Concepcion is delayed by

the reluctance of the priests to perform a marriage between the Roman Catholic Concepcion and the Russian Orthodox Rezanov without special permission from the Pope. The loading of the *Juno* is as hurried as the single available skiff will permit, and on May 10 she sails.

As she slips between the red rock cliffs at the mouth of the great bay, slapped heavily by whitecaps and slow to answer her helm, a family of sea lions frolics briefly alongside. The *Juno* reaches the open sea and turns to begin tacking northward along the coast. In her holds are 50 tons of grain, 9½ tons of tallow and butter, two tons of salt. In four weeks she makes landfall off Sitka. Guns are fired from shore in welcome, and a small boat, rowed by men as wasted as skeletons, pushes out from shore. In Rezanov's dispatch case is the plan for establishment of a Russian agricultural colony on the California coast to the north of San Francisco. He has seen the wilderness gentled, and he covets its fruitfulness.

November, 1841. They came tumbling down out of the mountains on foot and on horseback, thirty men and a woman with a child, ragged, exhausted, hurrying, strung out in a line four miles long. At a pond near the edge of the broad valley one of the men kills a coyote. So famished are these people that by the time the last man comes up, there are only a few guts left, and he devours them eagerly. He is a young man, big, a Missourian named John Bidwell, and like the rest he is near the end of his rope.

There had been sixty-nine in the party when they had set out from the Missouri River six months before to attempt the first overland immigration of American settlers into California. Though they had less than $100 in cash between them, they were well-outfitted with animals, wagons and supplies. They had read the letters of a former Missourian named Marsh describing the rich, untenanted lands of California, and listened to a trapper named Roubideaux talk of the healthfulness of the place.

They had traveled across country to the Platte in company with a party of missionaries and trappers bound for the Flathead country of the Rocky Mountains, and followed the Platte toward its western headwaters. They saw the Cheyenne, and herds of buffalo so incredibly vast that they galloped past their camp at full stampede for an entire night. Hail the size of turkey eggs fell to a depth of four inches on the plain, and waterspouts, willowy towers of wind-whipped moisture sucked up from the surface of the Platte, had bounced and danced across their trail. They had followed the Sweetwater to the foot of the Wind River Range, and crossed the Rockies at South Pass. They had forded the Green and camped to rest on the Bear. There the trappers and missionaries had turned north toward Fort Hall and the Snake. Half the immigrants went with them, abandoning their plan to reach California. Five of the prospective settlers were already dead or

turned back leaving thirty-two to press on west. All they knew was that California lay somewhere beyond the horizon.

They reached the Salt Lake in September, circled around it and kept on. In the desert they began to fear the approach of winter, so they abandoned the wagons, packing what they could carry on their animals and their own backs. Half the party was walking now, and the best packers took the lead, outdistancing the men who were forced to fuss and tinker with their packs.

They reached the Humboldt River and followed it downstream until it pooled and vanished in a broad tule marsh within an amphitheatre of gray sand and sagebrush. They could often see antelope browsing on distant hills, but could seldom steal close enough for a shot. They began slaughtering their oxen.

Traveling south and west they crossed the Carson and Walker Rivers, following the latter to where it emerged from a massive mountain range rising steeply up from the desert floor. Now very worried about their dwindling provisions and the imminent winter snows, they had no choice but to hurry on. They pressed up into the pine forests, keeping to the course of the river nearly to the summit, tugging and coaxing their animals along with the greatest difficulty.

Beyond the summit they struck a small westward-flowing stream which they followed downhill with increasing difficulty. After several days, they found themselves stranded on a narrow promontory between two sheer-walled gorges. John Bidwell and Jimmy Johns took horses and scouted a way down. At a narrow ledge some distance from where their companions were waiting, the two men argued about calling them along. Johns insisted the trail could be managed, Bidwell that it could not. Johns fired his pistol, signaling the others to follow them, and plunged down the canyonside on a horse Bidwell later described as coming "as near to climbing a tree as any horse I ever knew." Johns made it down, but the rest of the party could not follow. They spent the hours until sundown struggling down to the stream far below on foot and bringing back water for the animals in cups, camp kettles, even their own boots, and prospecting the rocky crevices for sparse handfuls of grass for feed. The following morning they reversed their trail and, eight men to an animal, hauled them back out of the impasse one by one. By the time they found an easier way down they had eaten the last of the cattle. They shot crows to live, and a wildcat. They still had no idea how far ahead of them California lay, nor when the snows would come.

The few animals left to them were starving on their bleeding feet, and the men made meals of rodents as they continued their slow descent of the mountains. Beyond them to the west they could see a purple line of summits on the horizon and supposed that California lay farther still beyond them. Their minds were numb with fatigue and oppressed by the spectres of freezing and starvation. And at last they stagger out onto the broad level plain of the great valley.

After killing and eating the coyote, the party turns north toward a meandering line of trees marking a streambed. There they find wild grapes and kill two sandhill cranes and two antelope. The next day they kill fifteen deer and antelope and jerk the meat for provisions for the climb over the mountain range to the west. They hurry, hunger appeased, but more frightened than ever of the impending winter. Two scouts go out in advance to find the fastest way, and at nightfall only one returns. They have met an Indian on horseback, he says excitedly, and although they could understand nothing of what he said, or nearly nothing, he had worn a cloth jacket. Over and over he had pointed toward the largest of the western mountains and said what seemed to be "Marsh."

In two days the entire party is camped at the Marsh Rancho in the San Joaquin Valley, in the gently swelling foothills of the Coast Range, eating pork and tortillas furnished by their host, and looking wonderingly about them at the California they had traveled so far to reach.

The great central valley had suffered a long summer of severe drought, and the grasses lie dead and gray on the earth, yet there is game everywhere. Antelope, elk and deer number in the tens of thousands and flow across the valley floor in great bands. Nearly as many long-legged, skinny Mexican cattle graze among them. Bears lumber down out of the high country to nibble at the greenery in the tule marshes where, in winter, flocks of ducks and geese cover the ponds almost solidly. Coyotes range everywhere, and mountain lions pad silently down out of the foothills. Swans and sandhill cranes patrol the streams and rivers in which fish flip and flash, and condors hang motionless in the sky, save for a microscopic trembling.

In all of the great San Joaquin Valley there are three ranches, those of Marsh, Livermore and Amador, and one, Sutter's, in the lower Sacramento. Agriculture is limited to vegetable gardens and larger acreages of barley and wheat, all of which are worked by Indians. They plant in furrows scratched by foot-burner plows and sweep the topsoil back over the seed with brooms. When it ripens they harvest it with hand sickles and carry it on the backs to corrals where they spread it evenly on the hard-packed earth floor. They drive a band of half-wild Spanish horses into the corral, haze them into an hour's frantic galloping before setting them free again, and then rake out the threshed wheat. The Indians of the Sierra foothills sortie down to steal horses for food. They and the animal predators take large numbers, but the herds increase.

California is now Mexican territory, and most of the coastal strip from San Diego to Sonoma has been partitioned into large ranchos. The vast mission holdings have been confiscated and sold into private ownership. Some of the missions lie abandoned, slowly going to ruin, while villages have grown up around others. The 30,000 Indian neophytes, deprived of their ancestral lands and their mission lands as well, go into the pueblos to work as menials, or to the ranchos as vaqueros. The great ranchos are as close to self-supporting as the large and industrious Indian labor force can make them. There is little cash in California, and the principal export is still hides and tallow. Trading ships from Boston call at the coastal anchorages to pay a dollar for each folded and tied hide, which have come to be called "California banknotes." The cattle carcasses are left in the interior to rot on the ground.

Government authority is only lightly exercised in California, and the rancheros live like feudal lords. They are generous, proud and improvident. A man traveling in California needs only a blanket and a knife— for these items are in short supply—and he may go where he pleases. There are no hotels or inns in California, and no need for them. Horses are abundant, and a man can take the one he wants simply by grabbing hold of the rope left trailing round its neck. He may ride twenty or thirty or fifty miles to the next rancho and exchange it for another simply for the asking.

John Bidwell is hired by Sutter, a man of preposterous generosity, to dismantle the Russian settlement at Fort Ross, which had been established in 1812 despite the death of Rezanov in Siberia the winter following his departure from San Francisco. Among the materials he transports to Sutter's Fort near the junction of the Sacramento and American rivers is a collection of French muskets believed to have been left behind in Napoleon's retreat from Moscow.

Bidwell's party is the first, but more are coming. In the next year alone there will be 250 American settlers entering California, drawn by the vision of a potential paradise. Among them will be a master carpenter named John Marshall.

July, 1852. The wooden semaphore arm on Telegraph Hill flips upward to signal the arrival of yet another ship carrying adventurers from the east, and yet another vessel slips into the naked forest of varnished spars rising starkly up from the innumerable ships anchored in San Francisco Bay. Small boats scull quickly out from shore to ferry passengers, baggage and cargo ashore at Long Wharf, and when a short, burly man with a broken nose, his two sons behind him, steps out of one of them, a brass band breaks into a thumping "Oh, Susanna!" Tom Maguire, San Francisco's leading impresario and proprietor of the famous Jenny Lind Theatre, leads a swarm of actors, actresses and stage hands to greet the three men, and to lead them along the crowded dock to a waiting carriage.

They clamber in with Maguire and the carriage lurches away from the busy harbor through dusty, windblown streets through which the people—and the rats—of five continents are moving. The ramshackle col-

woman clings to his arm, and as the men drift back from their panicked running into the forest, she glares at them defiantly. In this man's free hand is a bloody knife. At first the miners hang back as he promenades threateningly and boldly through the street; then six or eight men make a rush toward him. He is as quick. Leaving the woman and the knife behind, he whirls and dashes for the river, leaps into the current and swims strongly for the other side as it tugs him swiftly downstream. Shots are fired after him in a ragged volley, but he succeeds in reaching the far shore and sprinting to cover be-

down after it to continue digging toward bedrock.

If he is lucky, and can resist the epidemic discouragement, he will find a pocket of dust and nuggets in the stratum of tertiary gravel and clay resting on bedrock. If he is not lucky, the rains will come before he gets to it, and diggings will be impossible. He will leave the mines broke. And if he is unlucky, he will die.

Men are dying in the mines of typhoid and dysentery, from cave-ins and falls, from snakebite, starvation, ptomaine and alcoholism. They get rheumatism from standing

With an eccentric flourish the band completes its braying and the musicians take their instruments into the station. More prospective real estate speculators follow them than can squeeze into the waiting

to a harbor catering to ceaseless international trade, parade along the curving coastline. In Los Angeles alone, where the population has exploded from barely more than

lection of hovels that sprang up in the glory days of '49 have given way, in the aftermath of fire after disastrous fire, to substantial buildings of brick and dressed stone, even of iron. A steam locomotive chuffs toward them, carrying fill from the sand hills southwest of the city to the rapidly disappearing cove that indents the bay at the foot of Telegraph Hill. Some signs of the haste with which the city was settled still remain: the ships Apollo and Niantic serve as saloon and warehouse respectively, beached on what was once the shore, and is now several blocks from the water. The upper reaches of Telegraph Hill are aflutter with the rag-and-

any number of undiagnosed illnesses before they had even reached California, much less the gold fields. And when a ship did come, there was a ferocious rush to obtain the available space. Because of his fame, perhaps, or his supreme confidence, the elder Booth had managed to secure a cabin after only a brief wait.

Unfortunately for the Booths, the Jenny Lind is sold for use as the San Francisco City Hall, and they must close their performances after only two weeks of playing to an enthusiastic overflow audience. They depart for Sacramento.

Sacramento, a ten-hour steamer trip away,

waist-deep in the cold running streams all day long, and ophthalmia from the ever-present dust and the evaporating mercury in the gold recovery process. There are few doctors, and many of them are quacks whose

the brown plain, few of them more than a single story high. Beer, vinegar and wines are being produced in small quantities, but cattle represent the only significant industry. The heads, hooves and guts of slaughtered

Less than 25,000 descendants of California's Indian population remains.

Among more than a million residents of Los Angeles, 427,348 are church members, and the city ranks ninth in the nation in number of churches. But barely more than half of them are Roman Catholic or orthodox Protestant denominations. There are 204 branches of Aimee Semple McPherson's $1,500,000 Angelus Temple, and despite the scandal of her "kidnapping" in 1926, her church commands the spiritual allegiance of more than 16,000 souls. Almost as many are wearing I AM rings ($12) and poring over the materials contained in their special I AM Decree binders ($1.25), attending services of the Agabeg Occult Church, meetings of the Special Rose Light Circle, rituals of Mankind United, or sessions of the Self-Realization Fellowship of America where plans of a proposed $400,000 Golden Lotus Yoga Dream Hermitage are displayed.

San Francisco newspapers devote pages to the activities of the highly social First Families who own or control the real estate, industries and financial resources of the north. But in Southern California the social elite are not the First Families, who are scarcely known to the general public, but the movie people.

Movies had been made in California since 1908 when Col. William B. Selig finished his Count of Monte Cristo, begun in Chicago, on the shoreline at Laguna Beach. A few months later Selig's company built the first film studio in Los Angeles, a board-and-canvas lean-to behind a Chinese laundry on Olive Street, and in 1911 the first Hollywood studio was built by the Nestor Company at the corner of Sunset Boulevard and Gower Street. These early movie makers were the small independents who used bootlegged or pirated equipment in violation of patents issued to Thomas Edison and licensed to a limited number of major companies. They benefitted not only from the high number of sunny days and the variety of available scenery, but also from the proximity of the Mexican border and the haven it provided from process servers. So successful are they that the big companies follow them west. In time they become a major California industry, but their need for expansion capital brings eastern banks and corporations into ownership of the six biggest movie companies. Louis B. Mayer is the highest salaried executive in the United States.

In 1936, thirty-six years after the death of John Bidwell and twenty-five years after the last wild Indian in the United States is captured in a slaughterhouse corral near Oroville, there are more automobile fatalities in Los Angeles than in New York City. Paradise has swollen and taken on hellish and hallucinatory overtones.

On the eve of World War II California has recovered some of its economic strength. Aircraft manufacture is the principal industry of the state and only Detroit produces more assembled automobiles than the

cities, and are replaced in the fields by laborers from Mexico. When war comes, well-paying jobs are so plentiful that still another migration takes place into California, this one drawing heavily from the south and the southwest. In 1942 alone, 570,000 new citizens come to California to find work in the factories of war.

They build fighter planes and bombers at San Diego and Santa Monica, freighters and tankers at the newly-constructed shipyards on San Francisco Bay. They work in the Portland cement factories, in the state's first steel mills and in the iron mines in the Mojave Desert which supply them. Established industry retools and expands into war production: Yuba Consolidated Gold Fields Limited abandons the manufacture of gold dredging equipment to begin producing howitzers.

On the coast above San Diego 125,000 acres are made into a training facility for the Marine Corps. A huge tract near Monterey becomes the Army's Fort Ord. Navy establishments at San Diego and San Francisco are enlarged and increased. More than ten percent of the American armed forces train in California and a quarter of them make plans to return and settle in the state after their release from service.

At war's end heavy industry is a permanent addition to California's potent arsenal of attractions, and hundreds of thousands of citizens continue the westward flood. In 1962, less than 200 years after Serra had limped into the wretched camp at San Diego, California is the most populous state in the union.

Yet never once since 1848 have as many as half its residents been native-born.

The continuing stream of population into California is said to be the greatest mass migration of individuals in the history of the world. Moving west to California has become an American tradition, and California an eternal alternative—the land of new beginnings.

But because more than half its people have always been the restless and the ambitious, the breakaways and discards of a hundred different and conflicting traditions, there are lumps in the melting pot. California society is an uneasy coalition of strangers whose only shared tradition is a skepticism toward tradition, and it sometimes works awkwardly, as if held together with chewing gum and baling wire. It is no accident that the state which invented motels, supermarkets and gas stations also invented beatniks, hippies and Black Panthers.

California is still the tip of the American arrow. Less and less slowly and more and more surely all of us are wearing California clothing, thinking California thoughts—and facing California problems, and in that sense, California seems to be the ultimate destination for everyone.

No people in the history of mankind have ever lived the way Californians live today,

Right: Doves excitedly feed on grain around fountain in gardens of Mission San Juan Capistrano. In background is statue of Padre Serra, who founded this Mission on November 1, 1776. It is legendary for swallows to

acre, and there is no year in which some adventurous farmer does not discover some new product for which the climate and soil are especially adapted, and which pays better than gold mining." At night, after eating meals they had prepared for themselves on the cast-iron stoves provided for the purpose by the railroad, they bundled up in blankets or slept in their clothes on the narrow wooden cots made by folding down the seat backs in the coaches. Or they pace restlessly through the littered aisles from coach to frowsy coach, wondering if they have done right to give in to their restlessness and come west.

At one of the stations in the desert east of Los Angeles—Needles, perhaps—a Californian boards the train. As they rattle west through the Colorado desert the immigrants squint uneasily out at the barren landscape. When one of them turns to speak to the Californian, the journalist takes down their conversation:

"Anything grow along here?"

"Everything, sir, everything: the most productive soil on God Almighty's earth. All it wants is water."

"Fruits?"

"Fruits? I should say so. Every sort that's known. This country right here is going to beat the world in fruits."

"Melons?"

"Well, yes—no; the fact is, melons don't do so well here. They ain't apt to be good. The vines grow so fast that the melons are bumped along over the ground and bruised."

"Ah?"

"Yes...if you want to pick a melon in this country, you have got to get on horseback."

Now they stand on the railroad platform, hands rubbing uncertainly over stubbled chins and patting surreptitiously at the moneybelts around their waists. They stream out into the dusty street and blink back the bright mid-morning sunlight. The music of a brass band batters the cool, clean air, and leaflets are thrust into their hands. A painted billboard across the street shrieks silently at them: GLADSTONE!

Slowly they disperse, melting into the traffic of the city and moving in every direction. Wagonloads of lumber, brick and stone creak through swarms of lighter hacks and buggies. Another wagon, this one draped with bunting and carrying a brass band as cargo, wheels around the corner and rolls to a stop. Upright poles at each corner support banners reading GLADSTONE! And it is surrounded by people. The journalist is forced by the crush to stop and read the message painted in small letters along the bottom of the banner. "Free excursion to the new metropolis of the Azusa! Four coaches arranged! Departing the Santa Fe at 12:30 sharp! Lot auction! Free lunch! Free band concert!"

With an eccentric flourish the band completes its braying and the musicians take their instruments into the station. More prospective real estate speculators follow them than can squeeze into the waiting coaches. Curious and impressed, the journalist reaches into his pocket and pulls out the printed circular he had received at the railroad station, glancing down at the tiny print as he is jostled by the crowd. "GLADSTONE!" it begins. "...in the midst of the choicest orange groves and vineyards of that delightful section and in the natural center of trade and travel...the most perfect climate in California...all the streets will be graded and water is plentiful and abundant and will be piped to every lot...the First National Bank of Gladstone, which will be built of solid granite. A newspaper will be established at once...A valuable water power furnished from a fall 200 feet high... Hinda Villa Hotel now open...located on two lines of transcontinental railroad, both of which cross lands of the company."

Los Angeles is mad with real estate fever and Gladstone is only one of sixty new townsites platted between the San Bernardino Mountains and sea. The great Los Angeles basin is a pigmy forest of shin-high stakes

aflutter with knotted rags to mark off town lots, streets and avenues in grids across the rolling plain. Along the thirty-six miles of Santa Fe Railway track between the city limits of Los Angeles and the western boundary of San Bernardino County there are twenty-five new cities and towns. There are thirty-six in all in the San Gabriel Valley, and almost as many more, each with extravagant claims to a harbor catering to ceaseless international trade, parade along the curving coastline. In Los Angeles alone, where the population has exploded from barely more than

eleven thousand in 1880 to more than 80,000 in 1887, there are more than two thousand licensed land agents, each of them frenziedly selling townsite lots at prices that go up overnight. Gladstone! Pasadena! Bollona Bay! Santa Monica! Rosecrans! Ontario! Monrovia! Sunset! Long Beach! Recorded real estate transactions total about one hundred million dollars for the year, more than twenty-five times the aggregate bank assets only two years previously. And because deeds often change hands many times between issuance and recording, the actual sales total may be as much as $200,000,000.

It had started slowly enough back in the seventies. The rancheros who had managed

to keep title to their immense properties after statehood had prospered mightily during the livestock boom touched off by the gold rush. Their credit had never been better, and they had stretched it to the limit, spending freely everything they could borrow and earn. Their herds of skinny, long-legged Mexican cattle thrived in the golden valleys along the coast, and were tough enough to take to the thick brush of the mountains. In 1860 there were three million cattle grazing in California. 1862 was a drought year. 1863 was worse, and 1864 as bad. The cattle began dying of starvation and thirst, falling to their knees and unable to muster the strength to get up. Soon they were dying by the thousands, and at last whole herds, hundreds of thousands of animals, lay rotting in the back country. The stench of death was everywhere, and so sickening was it that the rancheros sent their vaqueros out to gather up the tottering rem-

nants of the great herds and drive them, staggering, into the sea.

The times were so hard in southern California then that no city taxes were collected in Los Angeles in 1864, and four business lots, offered at a tax sale for a total cash price of $2.50, went unbid. But by the seventies things were definitely improving. The population of Los Angeles had increased to more than five thousand. A railway connected the town with the port facilities at Wilmington. Horsecars carried passengers through a city still primarily Mexican adobe in architecture but with an increasing number of high-shouldered frame structures of Victorian design. In 1876 the Southern Pacific built its track through the wheat farms of the San Joaquin Valley to connect Los Angeles with San Francisco and with the east, and in so doing increased its holdings in California real estate to about ten million acres.

With eastern markets so much more accessible than by the old sea route around Cape Horn, southern California began to enjoy a mild prosperity again. Some of the old ranchos were subdivided into farming properties, and the farmers who came to take them up brought with them sophisticated irrigation techniques and a willingness to experiment with specialty crops. A slow transformation began to take place on the landscape: from open grazing of grassy hills and valleys, it became a crazy quilt of green plowed fields and belts of fruit trees. Three Brazilian orange trees were planted at Riverside in 1873 and their descendants soon replaced the sour, pulpy, thick-skinned descendants of the citrus fruit planted by the padres and which had found only a small market at San Francisco as a novelty item. Plums, peaches, apricots, walnuts, grapes, pears, olives and other crops were planted experimentally—even cotton and mulberries for silkworms. In 1884 California citrus swept the gold medals at the New Orleans International Exposition, and Southern California began to be regarded as a kind of terrestrial paradise.

When the Santa Fe finally succeeded in establishing its competing line into Los Angeles in 1885 the fuse started sputtering toward the boom. The railroads entered into a rate war, with one line bringing the fares down and the other undercutting it, until anyone could afford to come to California to see for himself. On one day in the spring of 1886 a man could buy a ticket to Los Angeles at Kansas City for a dollar, and though the price bounced up again the following morning, it stayed below $25 for several years.

Most of the people who come do so because of the glowing reports about the prosperity of southern California agriculture. As early as 1874 mature seedling orange trees were returning an average net profit to the grower of more than $20 per tree, or about $1500 per acre.

But as they search for temporary lodgings in the city jammed with immigrants, the newcomers begin to change their ideas. With so productive a land, and so many

people rushing in to fill it up, with the railroads and seaports to transport its produce to the great markets of the world—with every element necessary for success already at hand—perhaps it would be shrewder to defer the purchase of the small ranch or citrus grove until after the nest-egg brought from back home could multiply itself through investment in town lots. While agricultural acreage is slowly rising in price, town lots are increasing in value every day. Every Los Angeles business block is dominated by real estate offices, every conversation, no matter what the subject, veers inevitably to talk about land investment, every vacant patch of land carries a for sale sign, and every sale is made at a profit.

Examples of the inevitability of profit are commonplace, and are retailed freely in every house, every bar-room, on every street corner in the city. A man had bought thirty-two acres of empty ground at Vernon and Central Streets in 1883 for $12,000 and was lucky to get $8,500 for it two years later. But in 1887 a subdivider gives $40,000 for the property and considers it a bargain.

At Boyle Heights, near the new Santa Fe Depot, land sold for $5 and $10 an acre in the 1860's. In the early eighties individual lots there had brought as much as $150 and now some business locations are valued as high as $10,000.

At Azusa, west of Gladstone, eager buyers stand in line overnight to await the opening of the lot sales office. By morning the second man in line had refused $1000 for his place in line and the fifth man reluctantly accepts $500 for his. And why not? If he misses getting in on the ground floor at Azusa he can hardly fail to get in someplace else with prospects just as good.

The older settlers of the country are at first delighted at the sudden and unexpected demand for their land, and they make it available to subdividers at large and gratifying profits. Their delight then turns to amusement, amusement to contemplation, and contemplation to envy. They begin to buy back land, unwilling to see raw greenhorns make more for it than they had themselves.

THIS IS PURE GOLD!!
SANTA ANA,
The Metropolis of Southern California's
Fairest Valley!
Chief Among Ten Thousand, or the One
Altogether Lovely!
Beautiful! Busy! Bustling! Booming!
It Can't Be Beat!
The town now has the biggest kind of a
big, big boom.
A Great Big Boom! And You
Can Accumulate Ducats by Investing!

In April, recorded real estate transactions total more than $7 million, in June nearly $11 million, and in July nearly $12 million. The total since the beginning of the boom now exceeds two hundred million dollars, not counting unrecorded sales. So lucrative is the business of laying grids down upon the unused countryside that one promoter

beyond the San Bernardino Mountains, some fifty miles from Los Angeles itself, hangs oranges on Joshua trees and sells desert acreage as citrus groves. Another, only slightly closer in, lays down a line of fenceposts and declares the railroad will be completed as soon as the rails are received. Still another sells lots on a mountainside so sheer and worthless that he does not even bother to have them surveyed. He pays about 2¢ per lot for the land and gets in return anything from $1 to $250, according to what the market will bear. For obvious reasons he conducts his business by mail and does not advertise locally.

There is similar activity in San Diego, Ventura and Santa Barbara, but the center of excitement is Los Angeles. After touring the region and examining the boom, the journalist begins his article on the train home:

"It has been a subject of regret to me ever since," he writes, "that I did not buy Southern California when I was there last March, and sell it out the same month. I should have had enough to pay my railway fare back, and purchase provisions to last through the deserts of sand and feeding-places, and had money left to negotiate for one of the little states on the Atlantic coast, and settle down in such plain living and civilization as it might afford. It was all offered to me, but I hesitated, and before the end of the month it was beyond my reach."

Although few people have eyes for anything other than the great profits in Southern California real estate, San Francisco is growing as well. It is still the great city of the Pacific coast, already highly structured and hierarchical, and its growth proceeds at a more cautious pace.

Agriculture is transforming the great central valley of California. Wheat had been dry farmed there with good results in the 1860's, and by the seventies huge tracts were devoted to it. New laws make it the responsibility of the cattle ranchers to fence their herds, and across the crests of the low, rounded hills that bump up from the valley floor, combines, great clanking machines powered by steam and drawn by teams of as many as thirty-six horses, creep forward eighteen and twenty in a line into the deep fields of grain to chew a swath three hundred yards wide.

On John Bidwell's 20,000 acre Rancho Chico in the upper Sacramento Valley, the 1200 acres of orchards are thought to be the largest body of fruit-bearing trees on the Pacific Coast and perhaps in all the United States. He has 750 acres in alfalfa, and 200 to 300 acres more each year; 300 acres of raisin grapes, and 5,000 acres in wheat, oats and barley. On the rest he grazes sheep and cattle. He operates a dairy, a cannery, a soap factory, a flour mill and keeps chickens, turkeys and hogs, and his land reaches up from the bank of the Sacramento into the Sierra foothills.

These hills are empty now, or nearly empty, and the towns of the Mother Lode are husks. At Jimtown, Coloma, Fiddletown and Rough and Ready iron fire doors on unat-

tended stores with sagging ceilings hang open to the empty streets. In the larger towns, cities once, a faint village-sized pulse beats weakly at the dying heart, but the suburbs are atrophied and dead. Abandoned houses and cabins are taken apart for firewood. "The gold has gone," a newspaperman writes about Sonora. "In the frenzy of the earlier days, when millions were taken out every week; when the jail was as full as the mines; when on Sunday the miners formed a cue half a mile long, waiting for their letters at the post office; when every other house in the place was a bar-room or a gambling den; when Wells Fargo's strong box went down to Frisco daily with the ransome of an emperor—in the frenzy of those exciting times these elderly men spent their energies. They came to make their fortunes; those who succeeded went away to enjoy the prize; those who failed live on here, contented, thinking of the happy old days; with enough to eat, for living is cheap here, and no cold winters to dread, nor prosperous people to make them unhappy."

At Gold Run, at Smartsville, at Timbuctoo and at Rose's Bar there are still a few companies engaged in hydraulic mining, using high-pressure hoses to wash away whole hillsides at the rate of half a dozen acres a day. But the muddy runoff is damaging the farmlands of the Sacramento Valley, and they are forced to suspend operations. Gold mining is almost a dead letter in California now. Agriculture is boss, and the promise of paradise seems to have come true.

April, 1936. They come clattering out of the deserts in antique sedans and flapping-fendered pickup trucks bought from ruthless second-hand dealers back home. Front wheels nod crazily from side to side as the old crates churn along the lonesome straightaways and wheeze up the gentle slopes that separate the ash-heap mountains from one another. Tarps are tied loosely over stained, soggy mattresses laid flat on the roofs, and their frazzled ends snap dispiritedly in the mild flow of hot wind. Iron stoves are lashed to rear bumpers, and rotting steamer-trunks, and warped chests of drawers with the paint flaking off. Washtubs and disintegrating cardboard cartons are tied to the running boards, stuffed full of clothing, blankets, and bags of beans and flour. On the front bumpers, between the headlights, bald tires are braced against the groaning radiators.

Inside the cars are as many as eight, ten, even thirteen people, crammed in with all they own in the world: a box of cracked dishes and cheap forks and spoons, a few staple groceries, some shirts and coveralls, and, once in a while, a luxury. An old table radio, maybe, or a crank phonograph. These people are hot, tired and dirty. They are irritable. They are broke. They are hungry. They are desperate. And there are three hundred thousand of them in California.

Their desperation has been flowering for five years back in Oklahoma, Texas, Kansas and Colorado, beginning in 1931 when the bottom fell out of the price of wheat. 1932

was a drought year, and so was 1933. 1934 was another. And 1935. By then the rich farmland would barely grow weeds enough to support even a few scrawny cattle, and at last even they had to be shipped away to graze.

By then the winds had come to sweep across the plowed earth of the wheatfields and lift the topsoil into rolling clouds of dust. Months passed, years, and seldom a day when winds did not suck the soil up into the air to dim the sun. People took to taping their windows shut, and then to tacking them over with kerosene-sprayed bed sheets. But nothing they tried was enough to stop the steady, fine sifting of dust into the houses. On good days there was a little film of dust on the floors. On bad days it covered the floors in miniature rippling dunes. Outside huge drifts of dust built up to cover the Russian thistles until only a few protruding nettles poked through to the air. Fruit trees were buried to the tips of their twigs. Empty farmhouses were half-covered, and fences made long dikes of dust. People tied handkerchiefs over their faces to go outside, and daubed their nostrils with vaseline. In March of 1935 a seven-year-old boy suffocated in the dust near Hays, Kansas, and in April the dust was so thick in Texas the legislature met wearing gas masks.

Farmers failed. They waited for the rains to come, the winds to quit, and one by one they came to the end of their resources and had to quit waiting out the misery. Nearly ninety thousand square miles, part or all of sixty-eight counties in five states, became a barren bowl of dust. People are forced to leave.

Five years is a long time to get used to the idea of defeat, but these people are not used to it yet. This was their land; they are not drifters by nature. So shattered are they by the completeness of their failure that some even pull up the casings from their water wells to sell for scrap. No act of abandonment is as final in a land where water is so scarce. Mortgage holders foreclose the properties and bulldoze the fences and houses, but the people who have lived there do not stay to see it. They are long gone, gone to California.

Labor recruiters have passed through the country with news of work for men who know land and crops, and men take their families west to raise a little stake and put themselves back on their feet. But at the California border Los Angeles city police erect roadblocks, and from November, 1935, until April, 1936, they turn back any travelers who look as if they might turn up broke in L.A. The refugees veer south into Arizona, north to Colorado, Utah, Nevada, and back up as far as El Paso, Texas, until the roadblocks are abandoned and they begin streaming west again.

They reach the Imperial Valley, where water from the Colorado River irrigates huge tracts of reclaimed desert land planted in vegetables, lettuce, tomatoes and cabbage, and gives a yield of several crops a year. On the southern coast citrus groves deliver two

crops a year, but the picking season is brief. Dozens of crops are planted in the great central valley: cotton, grapes, beans, melons, peaches, pears, asparagus, walnuts, prunes. In the valleys of the north coast, lettuce, cauliflower, artichokes, apples and apricots flourish, and farther north there are grapes, hops, prunes and more. Thousands of men are required to harvest these crops, but not so many thousands as have come. In the last six months of 1935 alone, despite the road-blocks in November and December, more than 43,000 migrants were counted entering California in automobiles and trucks, and three-fourths of them are from the drought states to the east.

Like a rattletrap blitzkreig they make for the ripening fields. And they hurry, for they learn quickly that the growers advertise for more workers than they need in order to keep the wages low. They camp at the side of back roads, on the banks of irrigation canals, in Hoovervilles built of trash and weeds. Houses are constructed of flattened cans, cardboard, curling bits of scrap lumber, of tarps, or sheets and blankets hung from a line and staked at the corners with twigs. Toilets, where there are any at all, are holes in the ground surrounded by an apron of burlap tacked to a few wobbly posts. Water is dipped up from the canal. It is filthy, unhealthy and demoralizing. But it is free and these people have no money. They make do.

At some of the larger ranches there is housing available. Sometimes it is free, sometimes it must be rented for $3 or $5 a month. These are single room houses, usually about ten feet by twelve, bare-floored, with an iron wood stove as the only furnishing. Water is available from a spigot at the end of the row of shacks, and there is a single toilet for one hundred people. One Kern County ranch offers the luxury of a bath house: a single cold water shower to serve 400 people. Another big farmer refuses to provide water to the workers in his fields, but sells them lemonade for a nickel a glass. On some ranches there is a company store

that will advance credit for groceries to men who sign on for jobs. Otherwise there may be nothing to eat until the family starts earning its dribs and drabs of cash.

The lucky ones, the shrewd ones, the extra-energetic ones earn $400 in a year. Most earn much less—$150 with which to feed, clothe and transport their families to the next job. It is not enough. Many die, especially the children in whom illnesses are complicated by malnutrition. When anger and despair move the men to strikes, deputy sheriffs beat them, jail them, drive them out of the county. When they stage a march up the valley to Sacramento the municipalities along Highway 99 bring firetrucks to the edge of town and turn on the hoses to wash men, women and children into the ditches.

They are hated and despised, these people, for their frightening desperation is obvious. But they are needed, for without them the crops will go unharvested. So they are lured in great numbers to the harvest where they live in filth and work to exhaustion, and then they are chased away. They get what medical care they can afford, and they can afford little. Free services are reserved for local citizens, and even those few migrants who might be eligible for help do not know how to get it and are not encouraged to find out. They die of want at the edge of fields fat with food.

And in mid-January the work gives out altogether. The rains come, continuing until the middle of April when the wild grasses stand high in the fields, and orchards and vineyards are ready for the plow. The migrants build "Little Oklahomas," shanty-towns on the outskirts of Bakersfield, Fresno, Stockton, Marysville. They patch their wretched hovels with rags and weeds and mud, and wait out the rains.

If waiting becomes impossible, they give up and go to the cities. But there are already 25,000 drifting men lying up in Los Angeles, 40,000 more in San Francisco, and more yet in the smaller cities. Some towns put them to one kind or another of public work, but others are fearful. "One meal, one bunk, goodby" is the policy at San Luis Obispo; "Feed them and pass them on" at Ontario; "No assistance given" at Gardena; "No plan" at Huntington Beach. Nor is there any help at Gladstone: barley is growing where the eager lot buyers had picnicked fifty years earlier, and the boundary stakes rotted to nothing and plowed under.

It is not only the unemployed who have drifted west; the sick and the old have come, too. At San Diego, California's sunniest coastal city, 25% of the population is classified as sick or infirm, compared with a national average of 6%. The *Townsend Weekly* is read by 100,000 Californians who support the Old Age Revolving Pension Plan by sending its founders $950,000, most of it in nickels and dimes. Radio station KMTR is favorite listening for thousands more. It carries the broadcasts of Robert Noble, originator of the $25-Every-Monday pension plan that grows into the $30-Every-Thursday Ham & Egg movement.

Less than 25,000 descendants of California's Indian population remains.

Among more than a million residents of Los Angeles, 427,348 are church members, and the city ranks ninth in the nation in number of churches. But barely more than half of them are Roman Catholic or orthodox Protestant denominations. There are 204 branches of Aimee Semple McPherson's $1,500,000 Angelus Temple, and despite the scandal of her "kidnapping" in 1926, her church commands the spiritual allegiance of more than 16,000 souls. Almost as many are wearing I AM rings ($12) and poring over the materials contained in their special I AM Decree binders ($1.25), attending services of the Agabeg Occult Church, meetings of the Special Rose Light Circle, rituals of Mankind United, or sessions of the Self-Realization Fellowship of America where plans of a proposed $400,000 Golden Lotus Yoga Dream Hermitage are displayed.

San Francisco newspapers devote pages to the activities of the highly social First Families who own or control the real estate, industries and financial resources of the north. But in Southern California the social elite are not the First Families, who are scarcely known to the general public, but the movie people.

Movies had been made in California since 1908 when Col. William B. Selig finished his *Count of Monte Cristo,* begun in Chicago, on the shoreline at Laguna Beach. A few months later Selig's company built the first film studio in Los Angeles, a board-and-canvas lean-to behind a Chinese laundry on Olive Street, and in 1911 the first Hollywood studio was built by the Nestor Company at the corner of Sunset Boulevard and Gower Street. These early movie makers were the small independents who used bootlegged or pirated equipment in violation of patents issued to Thomas Edison and licensed to a limited number of major companies. They benefitted not only from the high number of sunny days and the variety of available scenery, but also from the proximity of the Mexican border and the haven it provided from process servers. So successful are they that the big companies follow them west. In time they become a major California industry, but their need for expansion capital brings eastern banks and corporations into ownership of the six biggest movie companies. Louis B. Mayer is the highest salaried executive in the United States.

In 1936, thirty-six years after the death of John Bidwell and twenty-five years after the last wild Indian in the United States is captured in a slaughterhouse corral near Oroville, there are more automobile fatalities in Los Angeles than in New York City. Paradise has swollen and taken on hellish and hallucinatory overtones.

On the eve of World War II California has recovered some of its economic strength. Aircraft manufacture is the principal industry of the state and only Detroit produces more assembled automobiles than the plants in California. The migrant families find jobs growing more plentiful in the cities, and are replaced in the fields by laborers from Mexico. When war comes, well-paying jobs are so plentiful that still another migration takes place into California, this one drawing heavily from the south and the southwest. In 1942 alone, 570,000 new citizens come to California to find work in the factories of war.

They build fighter planes and bombers at San Diego and Santa Monica, freighters and tankers at the newly-constructed shipyards on San Francisco Bay. They work in the Portland cement factories, in the state's first steel mills and in the iron mines in the Mojave Desert which supply them. Established industry retools and expands into war production: Yuba Consolidated Gold Fields Limited abandons the manufacture of gold dredging equipment to begin producing howitzers.

On the coast above San Diego 125,000 acres are made into a training facility for the Marine Corps. A huge tract near Monterey becomes the Army's Fort Ord. Navy establishments at San Diego and San Francisco are enlarged and increased. More than ten percent of the American armed forces train in California and a quarter of them make plans to return and settle in the state after their release from service.

At war's end heavy industry is a permanent addition to California's potent arsenal of attractions, and hundreds of thousands of citizens continue the westward flood. In 1962, less than 200 years after Serra had limped into the wretched camp at San Diego, California is the most populous state in the union.

Yet never once since 1848 have as many as half its residents been native-born.

The continuing stream of population into California is said to be the greatest mass migration of individuals in the history of the world. Moving west to California has become an American tradition, and California an eternal alternative—the land of new beginnings.

But because more than half its people have always been the restless and the ambitious, the breakaways and discards of a hundred different and conflicting traditions, there are lumps in the melting pot. California society is an uneasy coalition of strangers whose only shared tradition is a skepticism toward tradition, and it sometimes works awkwardly, as if held together with chewing gum and baling wire. It is no accident that the state which invented motels, supermarkets and gas stations also invented beatniks, hippies and Black Panthers.

California is still the tip of the American arrow. Less and less slowly and more and more surely all of us are wearing California clothing, thinking California thoughts—and facing California problems, and in that sense, California seems to be the ultimate destination for everyone.

No people in the history of mankind have ever lived the way Californians live today, and their way of life seems outlined on the horizon for us all.

Right: Doves excitedly feed on grain around fountain in gardens of Mission San Juan Capistrano. In background is statue of Padre Serra, who founded this Mission on November 1, 1776. It is legendary for swallows to return here each year on St. Joseph's Day.

Below: Waves of ever restless Pacific Ocean roll endlessly against the scenic shoreline of La Jolla.

Right: Lacy lichen drapes itself over stately oak tree in San Ynez Valley northwest of Santa Barbara.

Below: Attractive homes ring Avalon Bay, mecca for boaters, on Santa Catalina Island. Passenger ferry makes frequent trips from the Port of Long Beach.

Right: Fiery ball of the setting sun reflects its blazing color on the gentle shores of Corona del Mar.

Below: Hundreds of pleasure boats find fun in Newport Harbor surrounded by the communities of Newport Beach, Lido Isle, Linda Isle and Balboa Island.

Right: Afternoon sunlight shimmers across the Pacific as sailboaters enjoy their sport off Newport Beach. On Pages 36 and 37 following, playful children trying to capture sea gulls on southern California beach.

Right: Early morning fog drifts through a dense grove of graceful eucalyptus trees to form a mystic mood.

Below: Marineland of the Pacific, popular showplace of marine life located on the tip of the Palos Verdes peninsula. This aerial view shows the numerous pools, amphitheaters and revolving observation tower.

Right: Brilliant afternoon sun highlights pleasure boats on the rippled waters of Santa Barbara Harbor.

Below: The towers of Mission Santa Barbara at night. Late afternoon sun silhouettes a cluster of palm trees along Cabrillo Boulevard in Santa Barbara. Nearby, shore birds seek tasty morsels at the edge of the surf.

Right: Afternoon sunlight, rain clouds dramatically illuminate boats moored in Santa Barbara marina.

Below: Sun and fog combined create a spectacular image above Santa Ynez Valley in southern California.

Right: Moreton Bay fig tree roots developed a grotesque pattern in downtown city park, Santa Barbara. This fig tree, a native of Australia, was planted in 1877.

45

Right: Highway 1 spans the mouth of Rocky Creek along the spectacular and unspoiled Big Sur coastline.

Below: Headlands and coves form Big Sur country as it sweeps north along the coast for hundreds of miles. A lonesome cypress losing the struggle for survival in a secluded cove—Point Lobos Reserve State Park.

Right: Salmon Creek Falls makes a dramatic drop in the Santa Lucia range, Los Padres National Forest.

Below: Foaming surf washes sands of Carmel River Beach State Park. Pinnacle Rock viewed through arch of Monterey Cypress and fascinating patterns of surf-pounded sandstone in Point Lobos Reserve State Park.

Right: Magnificent hillside homes command spectacular view of surf and coastline near Carmel Highlands. On Pages 52 and 53 following—Offshore winds spin off crests of breakers rushing toward Monterey coast.

Below: Once standing Monterey cypress silhouetted against a colorful sunset on 17 mile drive near Carmel.

Right: Surfbound Pebble Beach Golf Course on the Monterey Peninsula, site of Bing Crosby Tournament.

Below: Giant Pacific breaker seems to explode as it crashes over rock along 17 mile drive north of *Carmel.*

Right: Spinach under irrigation in the heart of rich Salinas Valley. U. S. Highway 101 traverses this area.

Below: The "Sermon on the Mount" is portrayed in tile on the facade of Stanford University's Memorial Chapel. The thousands of minute pieces each were numbered prior to shipment from Italy for reassembly in this masterpiece at the famous chapel, *Palo Alto.*

Right: Rare mood of downtown San Francisco and the Bay Bridge captured from Yerba Buena Island as the sun slowly settles toward the Pacific Ocean. The bridge and its approaches stretch for eight miles.

Below: Scores of close fitting multiple dwellings huddle together on one of many hills of San Francisco; towers of the business district are on the skyline.

Right: Late evening sun partially silhouettes the campanile of the University of California at Berkeley.

Below: Downtown skyline of Oakland, California, reflected on surface of 155 acre Lake Merritt at dusk.

Right: Huge breakers dominate Point Reyes National sea shore seen from lighthouse north of San Francisco.

Below: The "Great Highway" at the western edge of San Francisco parallels the Pacific for many miles. Still standing as a reminder of past glories of the Panama-Pacific Exposition of 1915, is the restored palace of Fine Arts. Coit Tower high atop Telegraph Hill and sailboat gliding across the water of San Francisco Bay are areas of interest in this famous city.

Right: Brilliantly colored grape foliage marks entrance to Christian Brothers Wine Cellar at St. Helena.

Below: Picturesque Mt. Tamalpais State Park offers commanding view of surrounding hills and Pacific Ocean north of San Francisco. Two hundred acres of vineyards, viewed from the air and at ground level, surround Mont La Salle Novitiate and Winery in California's Napa Valley. It is owned and operated by the Christian Brothers who came to California in 1868.

Right: Napa Valley vineyard and walnut orchard combine to form a brilliant display of scenic beauty.

Right: Similar views may be seen from many shore-side parks along Sonoma County coastal headlands. Hillside homes hug the shoreline near Bodega Bay.

Below: Reconstructed facsimile of Russian Chapel at historic Fort Ross. Mouth of Noyo River offers snug retreat for commercial fishing fleet near Fort Bragg.

Right: Brood mares and their colts graze on rolling pastureland in a northern California inland valley.

Below: Winter sun silhouettes old oak tree in northern California. Picnicking amidst giant redwoods beside the Eel River in northern California. Fishermen and sea gulls reap a rich harvest of candlefish as they enter mouth of Redwood Creek near Eureka. These smeltlike fish invade the river mouth each spring.

Right: Autumn's brilliant colors reflected on the Russian River paralleling U.S. Hwy. 101, south of Ukiah.

Right: This well preserved Carson House in Eureka is perhaps one of California's most picturesque homes. It is now a private club for members and their guests.

Below: Spring blooms on native rhododendron in Redwood Creek area of Redwood National Park. Five-finger fern on walls of Fern Canyon. Coastal elk herd appears very docile as it grazes near Prairie Creek.

Right: Spectacular view in Jedediah Smith redwood preserve at northern tip of Redwood National Park.

Below: Cresting wave enveloping offshore rock along Del Norte coastline a few miles south of Crescent City. Memorial lighthouse at Trinidad on northern California coast. Picturesque coastline of Mendocino County.

Right: A brilliant sunset reflects on Pacific breakers along the Del Norte Coastline in northern California.

Below: Autumn foliage and evergreen forests surround rugged granite peaks of Castle Crags State Park.

Right: Burney Creek drops 132 feet over a lava wall in McArthur-Burney Falls State Park off State Hwy. 89.

Below: Kings Creek cuts through melting snow to form a cataract in Lassen Volcanic National Park. Snow geese and a few Canada geese were startled by the photographer at Tule Lake Wildlife Refuge. Blazing star wildflower in northeastern *California*.

Right: Cluster of Jeffrey pine cones in Lassen Volcanic National Park. They average 4″ to 6″ in diameter. On pages 84 and 85 following: Thousands of ducks and geese take to air above Tule Lake Wildlife Refuge. The white birds are the famed Snowgeese. In foreground, grain fields planted just for their benefit.

Right: A duck hunter and his dog head out into the marshland of Tule Lake, California. Large areas of this refuge are open to hunting, situated in the Klamath basin of northern California and southeastern Oregon.

Below: Shasta Dam on the Sacramento River. It impounds 55-mile-long Shasta Lake, offering a wide variety of recreation. Mt. Shasta dominates horizon.

Right: Built of layered lava, Mt. Lassen, largest plug dome volcano in the world, rises to an elevation of 10,457 feet, some 4,500 feet above Manzanita Lake.

Below: A skier glides down a gentle southern slope in Mt. Shasta's ever popular winter recreation area.

Right: Ice melting in midsummer on Lake Helen near 9,000 foot elevation—Lassen Volcanic National Park.

Below: Lassen County's colorful Red Rock Canyon. Foreground, berries hang heavy on hardy juniper tree.

Right: Giant 6,907 foot high cinder cone dwarfs lonesome Jeffrey pine in Lassen Volcanic National Park.

Right: New growth on stalwart sage bush indicates a will to survive in Lava Beds National Monument area.

Below: Graceful symmetry of Capitol dome reflected in nearby pool. Sacramento, once the peaceful domain of Captain John Sutter, is the seat of State Government. Along Interstate 5 one of many rural reflections of the broad, fertile Sacramento Valley and from the air, rice fields form an interesting pattern.

Right: Feather River swirls over boulders on canyon floor at depth of 2,500 feet in lower gorge area.

Below: Mountain retreat in Twin Lakes area near Bridgeport. Looking west at the Sierra Nevada range, a gale force wind is blowing snow high into the sky.

Right: Raymond Meadow Creek follows rocky slope near summit of Ebbetts Pass in Sierra Nevada range. On pages 100 and 101 following—Winter reflection over Sawtooth Ridge and Twin Peaks in the high Sierras casts a brilliant glow on Twin Lake Reservoir. This natural beauty is part of Hoover Wilderness area.

Below: Expert skiers race down a slope at Squaw Valley, site of the 1960 Olympic Games. The girl at right proves male skiers have no corner on courage.

Right: Intricate patterns of ice, snow and water create unusual winter formation in the Sierra Nevada Range.

Below: Ranch in mid-winter along the Truckee River in the foothills of the Sierra Navada Range eastside.

Right: Western yellow pine appears to be winning the struggle for survival over glacial rock along middle fork of Stanislaus River Canyon near Dardanelle.

Below: Quaking aspen and rabbit brush forecast winter's coming to the Sierra Nevada Range eastside. Viewed at edge of Grant Lake on June Lake loop road.

Right: Winter storms prevailed as whitebark pine fought for survival. Green Lake, Mt. Conness (elevation 12,560 feet) and Conness glacier in background.

Right: Middle fork of Stanislaus River cuts through sheer glacial narrows near Dardanelle recreation area.

Below: Lake Sabrina in granite pocket. Distant peaks include Mt. Darwin in Kings Canyon National Park.

Right: Swimmers enjoying the crystal clear waters of Lake Tahoe. In background the Sierra Nevada Range.

Right: Sugar pine takes shape of an espalier against a mountain wall in the Desolation Valley Wilderness.

Right: Sawtooth Ridge in Twin Lakes area—Sierra Nevada eastside. Foreground, yellow Wyethia plant.

Below: Alpine pasture at the base of Sawtooth Ridge near Bridgeport on U.S. 395—Sierra Navada eastside.

Right: Near the crest of Carson Pass can be seen spectacular reflections of the Sierra Nevada Range.

Below: The Trinity Alps in mid-April. A brilliant California poppy often seen in many areas of the state. Formal plantings in Capital Mall surround the gold domed capitol building in downtown Sacramento.

Right: California's famed Central Valley in early morning. By means of irrigation this rich soil provides a wealth of tomatoes, melons and other produce.

Below: A new section of Interstate 5 sweeps across the 200 foot wide California aqueduct near the San Luis Reservoir. In background, the Delta Mendota Canal, another artery of this huge irrigation system.

Right: Tractor furrowing for irrigation water in Central Valley Reclamation area. Air view near Los Banos.

Below: Golden field of grass offers brilliant contrast to Mt. Tom in background—Sierra Nevada eastside.

Right: An Emerald lake reflects granite peak along middle fork of Bishop Creek—Sierra Nevada eastside.

Below: Old tailing wheels in the Mother Lode mining country along State Highway 49 north of Angels Camp. Tuolumne River flows over a natural granite stairway in Yosemite National Park. Small streams almost without number are found in the Minarets Wilderness area northwest of Bishop on U.S. 395.

Right: Seemingly immovable boulders appear small compared to Half Dome—Yosemite National Park.

Below: Nevada Falls on the Merced River in Yosemite National Park. Lightning creased Jeffrey pine atop Sentinel Dome. Upper Yosemite Falls drops 1,430 ft.

Right: Mt. Conness and Green Lake in the Hoover Wilderness bordering Yosemite National Park. Winds often contort the timberline trees into strange shapes like the fallen, weather-bleached Whitebark pine.

Below: The receding shores of Mono Lake. In background, peaks of Yosemite from left to right: The Koip Crest, Mt. Gibbs and Mt. Dana (elev. 13,050 ft.).

Right: Winter reflections on Merced River ahead of majestic Sentinel Rock in Yosemite National Park.

Below: Upper portion of El Capitan reflected in waters of the Merced River—Yosemite National Park.

Right: Winter's gentle face cloaks Half Dome rising 4,800 feet from the forested floor of Yosemite Valley. On pages 132 and 133 following: Winter sunset on El Capitan above the Merced River in Yosemite Valley.

Below: Cottonwood tree robed with autumn foliage in Owens Valley. Background, Sierra Nevada Range.

Right: Thousand Island Lake in Minarets Wilderness on the crest of the Sierra Nevada Range, at an elevation of about 10,000 feet. Banner Peak in background.

Below: Old tungsten mine no longer in use stands as a relic of the past in the White Mountains of eastern California. General Grant tree, known as the "nation's Christmas tree," in Kings Canyon National Park. It is one of the largest and oldest of all the giant Sequoias measuring 33 feet across at ground level.

Right: Church tower and tin-sided building in Bodie appear structurally sound in this semi-arid region.

136

Below: Autumn offers a rich contrast to the Sierra Nevada Range eastside. Behind cottonwood tree is 14,375 foot Mt. Williamson obscured by clouds.

Right: Copper Creek before it makes its entry into Zumwalt meadows and the south fork of Kings River.

Below: Lone Pine Peak and Mt. Whitney tower above Alabama hills in foreground—Sierra Nevada eastside.

Right: Middle fork of the Kaweah River tumbles over huge granite boulders in Sequoia National Park.

Right: Morning mist envelops a grove of giants in Sequoia National Park. Bracken ferns cover the earth.

Right: Sherman Creek winds its way through a forest of giants in 604 square mile Sequoia National Park.

Below: Stark contrasts of the desert. Lone Pine Peak above the Alabama Hills—Sierra Nevada eastside.

Right: Warm light shrouds snow-covered giants in Sequoia National Park. Some are over 3,000 years old. On pages 148 and 149 following: Thriving in desert heat, clump of Creosote stands alone as the sun rises over Mesquite Flat dunes in Death Valley National Monument. In background, the Grapevine Mountains.

Right: Contrasting white phlox and dolomite in ancient bristlecone pine area of White Mountains.

Below: Racetrack in Death Valley National Monument. Mystery surrounds the origin and movement of this lonesome rock. Gale winds may be responsible.

Right: Beavertail cactus and desert Aster give the arid Mojave Desert a touch of brilliant color in late May. In background are rolling Death Valley Buttes.

Right: Vegetation thrives in volcanic field at base of Ubehebe Crater. In background, Tin Mountain (elevation 8900 ft.) in Death Valley National Monument.

Below: Death Valley badlands with the Panamint Range on the horizon looking west from Zabriskie Point. Highlights and shadows grace the rippled Mesquite Flat dunes, Death Valley National Monument.

Right: Telescope Peak (elevation 11,049 ft.) reflected on the surface of Badwater. In this general area (282 feet below sea level) is the lowest point in the Western Hemisphere, Death Valley National Monument.

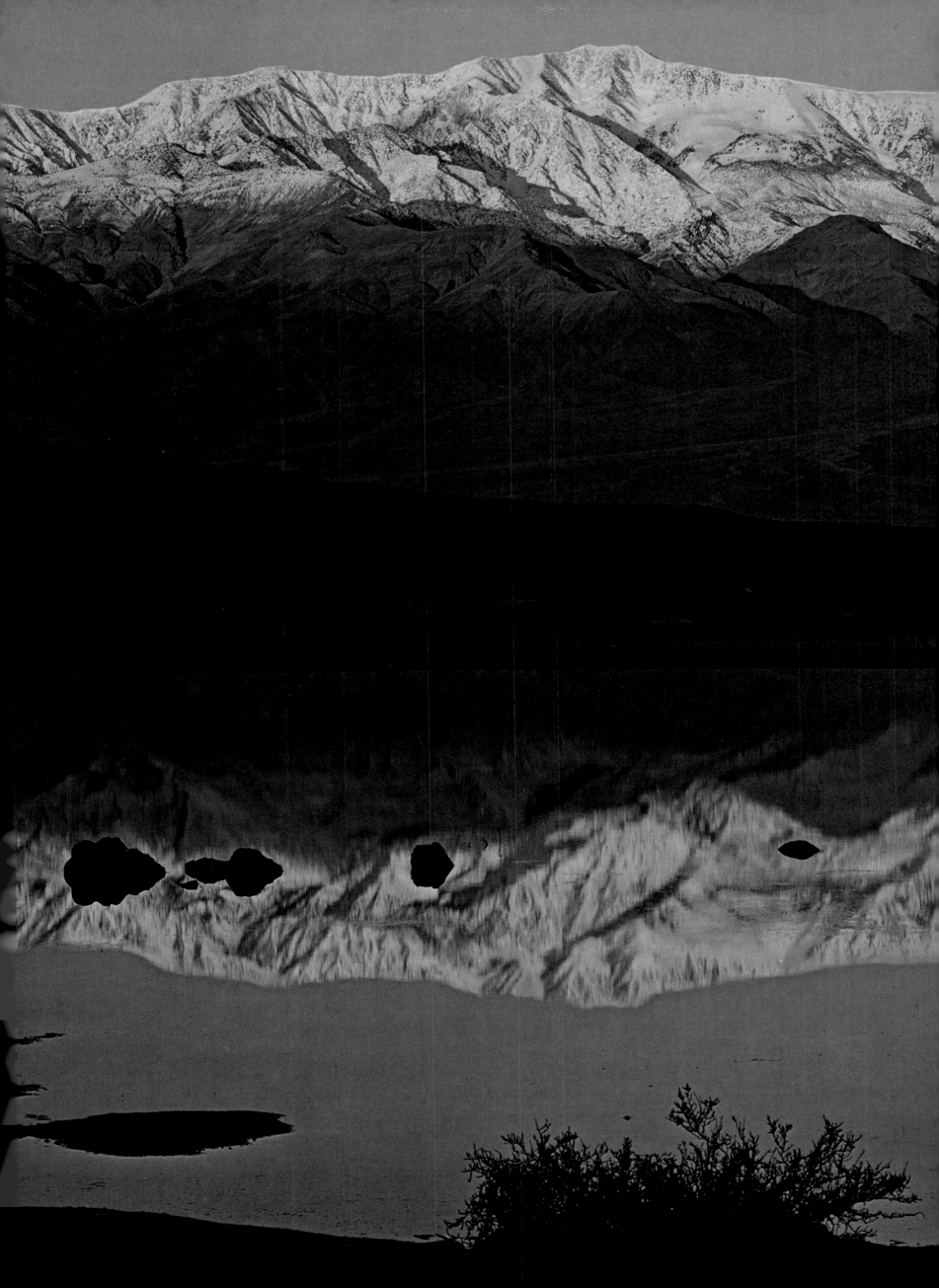

Below: Looking north from Dantes View into the wide expanse of Death Valley National Monument.

Right: Alkali cakes carpet desert floor near Mesquite flat dunes in the Death Valley National Monument.

Right: Shaggy, angular Joshua trees (members of the lily family) adapt to the higher regions of the Mojave Desert in Joshua Tree National Monument. In background, some large quartz monzonite formations.

Below: Winter's generous mantle gracefully adorns a cluster of Joshua trees and San Gabriel Mountains.

Right: Mt. San Jacinto gives cooling contrast to cacti entourage on Colorado desert near Palm Springs.

Below: Acres of young carrots growing in the mild climate of the fertile Coachella Valley of southern California. Crops can be planted almost any time in this area. This young crop was planted in November. In background Chocolate Mountains and Date Palms.

Right: Morning sun highlights yucca blooms at base of 10,831 foot Mt. San Jacinto in Colorado desert.

Right: Washingtonia palms line rocky canyon near Palm Springs. Trees reach average height of 50 feet.

Right: Satin smooth Taquitz Falls drops into a rocky
cavern near the popular resort area of Palm Springs.

Below: Date palms display their fruits as harvest time approaches near Palm Desert in the Coachella Valley.

Right: Vineyard under irrigation in fertile Coachella Valley at the base of the Santa Rosa Mountains.

Below: A grove of young Washingtonia palms in Borrego Palm Canyon—Anza Borrego Desert State Park. A foursome enjoying Indian Wells Golf Course, Palm Desert, California, site of the Bob Hope classic.

Right: Desert palm oasis in rock laden Borrego Palm Canyon. Foreground, Encelia and Chuparosa blooms.

Right: Borrego Springs Valley in Anza Borrego State Park. Foreground, Beavertail Cactus and Ocotillos.

Right: Carpet of Lavender Verbena dominates this colorful display on the Colorado desert near Borrego Springs. In background, the San Ysidro Mountains.

Below: A regimented formation of geese soar over thousands of snow geese on Tule Lake. They make up the many thousands of waterfowl that stop here for a period of feeding during their annual fall migration.

Right: Mission San Luis Rey near Oceanside. Brilliant color of prickly pear cactus enhances the beauty of this stately old mission founded on June 13, 1798. On pages 180 and 181 following: Cloud capped Mt. Shasta (elevation 14,162 ft.), the volcanic giant of northern California retaining unspoiled grandeur.

Below: Spring in San Rafael Wilderness foothills Santa Ynez Valley. Background, 6,000 foot McKinley Peak.

Right: Ever active sea gulls wheel and dive above the surf, seeking marine food at Point Sur south of Carmel. On crest of rock in background Coast Guard station.

Below: Venerable old Jeffrey pine determined to live forever atop Sentinel Dome, Yosemite National Park.

Right: Delicate Najoqui Falls in Los Padres national forest near the historic Danish community of Solvang.

Below: Foothills of the Diablo Range rise above the surface of San Luis Reservoir supplying irrigation water for the San Joaquin Valley. This reservoir was created by a mile long dam over 300 feet in height.

Right: Nevada Falls on the Merced River dwarfed by Liberty Cap and Half Dome in Yosemite National Park.